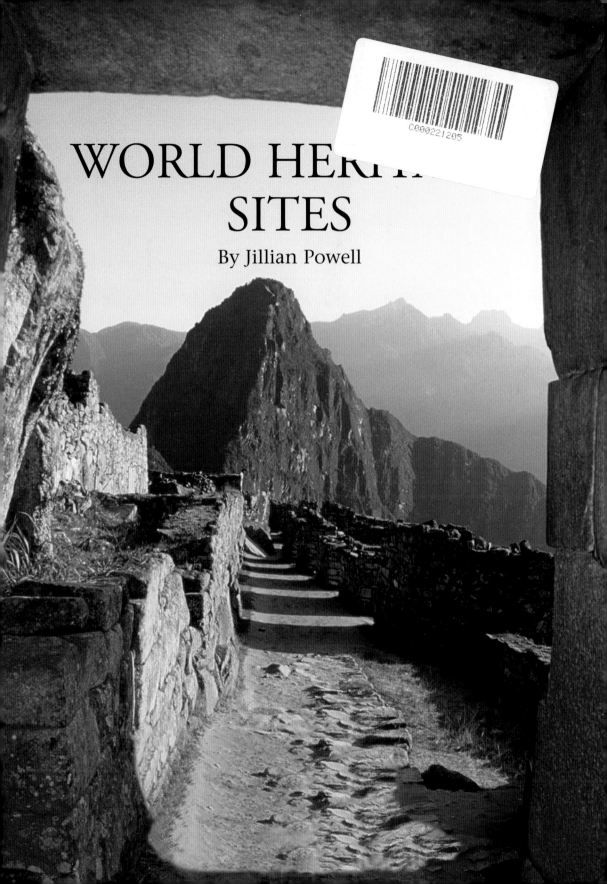

WORLD HERITAGE SITES

By Jillian Powell

Series Literacy Consultant
Dr Ros Fisher

Pearson Education Limited
Edinburgh Gate
Harlow
Essex CM20 2JE
England

www.longman.co.uk

ISBN 0 582 84134 8

Colour reproduction by Colourscan, Singapore
Printed and bound in China by Leo Paper Products Ltd.

The Publisher's policy is to use paper manufactured from sustainable forests.

The following people from **DK** have contributed to the development of this product:

Art Director Rachael Foster

Martin Wilson **Managing Art Editor**	**Managing Editor** Marie Greenwood
Emy Manby **Design**	**Editorial** Jennie Morris
Helen McFarland **Picture Research**	**Production** Gordana Simakovic
Richard Czapnik, Andy Smith **Cover Design**	**DTP** David McDonald

Consultant David Green

Dorling Kindersley would like to thank: Shirley Cachia and Rose Horridge in the DK Picture Library; Ed Merritt in DK Cartography; and Johnny Pau for additional cover design work.

Picture Credits: Corbis: Yann Artus-Bertrand 29br; Dean Conger 28; Michael Freeman 24b; Gallo Images 17bl; Michael John Kielty 25; Charles and Josette Lenars 26; Craig Lovell 15t; William Manning 30; James Marshall 12tl; Joe McDonald 6cr; Roger Ressmeyer 27b; Galen Rowell 1, 14b; Paul A. Souders 13; Keren Su 21b; Luca I. Tettoni 19t; Sandro Vannini 23; Julia Waterlow 27tr; Nik Wheeler 12b, 20tl; Jim Zuckerman 18. DK Images: National Trust/Andy Williams 8tr. Getty Images: Gary Bell 10–11; Richard Dobson 17bl; Orion Press 20b. Photolibrary.com: Demetrio Carrasco 6–7. Russia and Eastern Images: 11cr. Science Photo Library: Bernhard Edmaier 9. Cover: Getty Images: Kevin Schafer front t.

All other images: DK Dorling Kindersley © 2004. For further information see www.dkimages.com
Dorling Kindersley Ltd., 80 Strand, London WC2R 0RL

Contents

Great Pyramid of Giza

World Heritage Sites

A World Heritage Site is a place of worldwide importance. Each site belongs to the people of the world and every effort is made to preserve it for future generations.

There are hundreds of protected sites on the **UNESCO** World Heritage List. Every site has to be accepted before it is included on the list. First the government of the country in which the site is found explains to UNESCO's World Heritage Committee why the site should be protected. If the Committee agrees, then the site may become a World Heritage Site.

World Heritage Site Locations

This map shows you the World Heritage Sites that you can read about in this book.

NORTH AMERICA

Yellowstone National Park, USA

L'Anse aux Meadows, Canada

Grand Canyon National Park, USA

Equator

Angel Falls, Venezuela

Machu Picchu, Peru

Nasca Lines, Peru

Brasília, Brazil

Rapa Nui National Park, Easter Island

SOUTH AMERICA

Types of World Heritage Sites

mixed sites

cultural sites

natural sites

There are currently 730 sites on the World Heritage List – 563 are cultural, 144 are natural and 23 are mixed.

World Heritage Sites are natural or **cultural**. Natural sites include amazing mountain ranges and mighty waterfalls. Often they are a type of environment or a **habitat** for **endangered species** of wildlife or plants. Cultural sites have been shaped by people. They are places where we can learn about **civilizations** of the past. Some sites have both cultural and natural value.

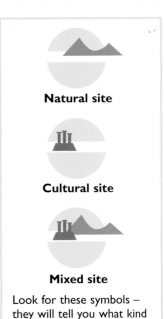

Natural site

Cultural site

Mixed site

Look for these symbols – they will tell you what kind of site you are reading about.

Giant's Causeway, Northern Ireland

Stonehenge, England

Windmills at Kinderdijk-Elshout, Netherlands

EUROPE

Lake Baikal, Russian Federation

Pont du Gard, France

Leaning Tower of Pisa, Italy

ASIA

Colosseum, Italy

Great Wall, China

Epidaurus Amphitheatre, Greece

Great Pyramid of Giza, Egypt

Giant Buddha of Leshan, China

Taj Mahal, India

Mount Everest, Nepal

Timbuktu, Mali

Rice Terraces of the Philippine Cordilleras, Philippines

AFRICA

Angkor, Cambodia

Equator

Serengeti National Park, Tanzania

Kakadu National Park, Australia

Great Barrier Reef, Australia

Mosi-oa-Tunya, Zambia and Zimbabwe

Uluru, Australia

Fossil Hominid Sites, South Africa

AUSTRALIA and OCEANIA

N

E

S

Fiordland National Park, New Zealand

ANTARCTICA

5

Rocky Places

Powerful natural forces, such as volcanoes and rivers, have shaped Earth's surface over billions of years. The rocky places on **UNESCO**'s World Heritage List help us understand Earth's long history and its future.

Grand Canyon National Park, USA

The Grand Canyon cuts through the Grand Canyon National Park in Arizona. From the rim of the canyon, the landscape extends as far as the eye can see. It is dazzling in colour, with rocks ranging from black to brilliant red and soft lavender.

American Bald Eagle

For the last 6 to 10 million years, the canyon has been slowly carved out from a flat area of rock by the powerful Colorado River. It is 445 kilometres long, 29 kilometres wide and 1.8 kilometres deep. Its rocks range from 250 million years old at the top, to more than 2 billion years old at the bottom. Some of its rock contains **fossils** of the earliest living creatures.

Today the Colorado River is still cutting down into the canyon's bed, and deepening it. Wind batters the rock face and carves out strange shapes. Water seeps into cracks in the canyon's rocks, then freezes and expands, forcing the rocks further apart.

Wind and weather have eroded the canyon.

Giant's Causeway, Northern Ireland

Legend says that a giant who lived in Northern Ireland built a path, or causeway, across the Atlantic Ocean to Scotland, to reach the female giant whom he loved. The Giant's Causeway was actually formed by an erupting volcano about 50 to 60 million years ago. As the **lava** cooled, it shrank and cracked to form more than 40,000 brown columns. These columns rise out of the sea as if designed to do so. The tallest column stands 12 metres high.

The Giant's Causeway's gigantic columns are made from cooled lava.

Uluru, Australia

Uluru is in the Uluru-Kata Tjuta National Park in the centre of Australia. It is a vast red sandstone rock that rises 348 metres above the flat desert. Uluru is famous for its vibrant colours that change as the Sun reflects on different minerals in the rock. Uluru is also a sacred site for Australian Aboriginals. Their carvings and paintings decorate ledges and caves inside some parts of the rock.

Uluru is a sacred site for Australian Aboriginals.

Watery Places

Water forms roaring waterfalls, deep lakes and steaming hot **geysers** that bubble out of the ground. Rivers, lakes and oceans also provide habitats for many **endangered species**.

Yellowstone National Park, USA

Yellowstone National Park in Wyoming has more geysers than anywhere else on Earth. This is because the park lies on a "hot spot" – a chamber containing hot **molten** rock that has erupted from deep inside Earth. When water trickles underground and meets this rock, it is heated to boiling point and changes into steam. This steam rises and gets trapped in channels leading to the surface. Then the pressure of the steam builds up until it forces the water out of the ground as a spectacular geyser. Yellowstone National Park also contains about 10,000 other types of water feature that are warmed by the Earth's inner heat.

This geyser is called Old Faithful because it erupts so frequently.

Great Barrier Reef, Australia

The Great Barrier Reef is the longest coral reef in the world. It stretches for 2,027 kilometres along Australia's north-eastern coast. The Great Barrier Reef is made up of many coral reefs that form a barrier between the coast and the Pacific Ocean. A coral reef is made from the bodies of living and dead coral. There are about 400 types of coral in the Great Barrier Reef. They come in many shapes and sizes. Some look like delicate fans and feathers, while others look like exotic flowers or miniature trees.

Coral reefs have been called "the tropical rainforests of the ocean" because of the variety of life they contain.

Live coral are richly coloured. As they die, they leave behind white chalky skeletons. The Great Barrier Reef is also home to 1,500 species of fish and is the **habitat** of **endangered species** such as the green turtle.

Lake Baikal, Russian Federation

Lake Baikal has a wide range of animals in its waters.

At 25 million years old, Lake Baikal is the oldest lake in the world. At 1,637 metres deep, it is also the world's deepest lake. More than 300 rivers and streams flow into Lake Baikal, and it holds a fifth of all the unfrozen fresh water in the world. Many species are only found in the lake, such as omul salmon and nerpas, which are freshwater seals.

Angel Falls, Venezuela

In 1935 an American pilot called Jimmie Angel was flying over the remote mountains of south-eastern Venezuela. He landed his plane in search of gold, but found something more exciting – the highest waterfall in the world. Jimmie probably heard the waterfall before he saw it. Water roars and thunders down the sheer vertical edge of a **table mountain** called Auyantepui. Angel Falls forms part of Canaima National Park.

Water at Angel Falls cascades 807 metres down Auyantepui Mountain.

Mosi-oa-Tunya, Zambia and Zimbabwe

Mosi-oa-Tunya means "the smoke that thunders". The name describes the shimmering mist and spray rising from this waterfall, which can be seen from 20 kilometres away. Mosi-oa-Tunya is also called Victoria Falls. It is fed by the Zambezi River, which is more than 2 kilometres wide at the point where it noisily plunges over the falls.

At the height of the rainy season, the Zambezi River pours more than 500 million litres of water over the edge of Mosi-oa-Tunya every minute.

Wild Places

Some environments in the world are still wild and unspoilt. They are protected by **UNESCO** because of their beauty and for their importance for native animal and plant species.

Fiordland National Park, New Zealand

Fiordland's wild landscape on New Zealand's South Island has been shaped over 500 million years by the movement of vast **glaciers**, and it is still changing today. Millions of years ago ice-age glaciers carved out five huge lakes and formed deep valleys. When the ice melted, the sea flooded into these valleys to form fiords – long, narrow inlets between steep slopes.

Fiordland is a remote area, surrounded by high mountains and covered in forest. It provides a **habitat** for many native species of wildlife including the Fiordland crested penguin and the takahe, a large flightless bird.

Milford Sound fiord in Fiordland National Park is 12 kilometres long and 320 metres deep in places.

Mount Everest, Nepal

Mount Everest lies in the Himalayan mountain range between Nepal and Tibet. It is the highest mountain in the world, standing almost 9 kilometres above sea level. Mount Everest forms part of Sagarmatha National Park – an area full of high mountains, deep valleys and **glaciers**.

About 70 million years ago Everest lay below the sea. Then about 30 million years later movements in Earth's **crust** began to create the Himalayas.

Mount Everest

In the Himalayas the temperature rarely rises above freezing, and so the tops of its mountains are always covered in snow and ice.

More than a million wildebeest migrate across the Serengeti at a time.

Serengeti National Park, Tanzania

Serengeti National Park in Tanzania covers more than 14,000 square kilometres of **savannah** that have hardly changed in the last million years. More than 3 million large mammals live in this hot, grassy **habitat**. Most of these animals only eat plants. They migrate in vast herds at different times of the year to find fresh grass and water. Other animals that live in the Serengeti include predators such as cheetahs and leopards, and large mammals like elephants and black rhinoceroses.

cheetah

Early Human Sites

Places where early people lived sometimes contain **fossil** remains such as bones, and ancient artworks such as cave paintings. These places show us how people lived thousands of years ago, including how they farmed the land and made shelters.

Kakadu National Park, Australia

Kakadu National Park in Australia's Northern Territory covers 20,000 square kilometres and includes tropical forests, soaring sandstone cliffs, crashing waterfalls and vast swamps. As well as being an area of natural beauty, the park is also an important **cultural** site.

Australian Aboriginals have been living in Kakadu for thousands of years.

Australian Aboriginals have lived on this land for more than 40,000 years. There are more than 7,000 examples of their rock art in the park's caves and alcoves. These include some of the world's oldest-known paintings, which were made more than 20,000 years ago.

Aboriginal rock art at Nourlangie Rock, Kakadu

Fossil Hominid Sites, South Africa

A group of sites in South Africa have been called "The Cradle of Humankind". **Archaeologists** believe that the first human beings, known as hominids, lived here. They have found many important clues to our past in caves in Sterkfontein, near Johannesburg. These include the fossilized remains of early hominids, as well as animals, plants and pollen. Archaeologists have also found some of the earliest-known stone tools made about 2 million years ago. One of the Sterkfontein Caves' oldest finds is "Little Foot", an incomplete skeleton believed to be 3.3 million years old. This skeleton was found in 1978, but was not recognized as a hominid until 1994. Archaeologists named it "Little Foot" because they found the foot first.

Caves in Sterkfontein have produced many archaeological finds.

"Little Foot" skull

Cities and Settlements

Some city and settlement sites on the World Heritage List are ancient remains that show us how earlier peoples laid out their cities, and what buildings they used. Other sites are cities where people still live and work. These sites are outstanding examples of town planning and building design.

Machu Picchu, Peru

Nestling high in the Andes Mountains are the ruins of the Inca city of Machu Picchu. The people who once lived here had natural springs for water, terraces for growing food and a city that contained palaces, temples, homes and public baths. They built their walls, terraces and ramps using blocks of stone cut from the mountains. Machu Picchu was deserted in the 16th century and was quickly covered by forest. It was rediscovered by an **archaeologist** in 1911.

About 10,000 people lived in Machu Picchu before it was deserted in the 16th century.

Angkor, Cambodia

The ancient city of Angkor has been called "the City of Temples" and contains the remains of more than a hundred magnificent temples. The temples house many beautifully carved statues and sculptures. Angkor Wat is the best-known temple. It was built in the 12th century.

Angkor has become one of **UNESCO**'s most endangered sites. Many of its treasures have been damaged or stolen.

L'Anse aux Meadows, Canada

In AD 985 sailors aboard an Icelandic trading ship saw new lands to the west. About fifteen years later Viking ships returned to Newfoundland and settled on its tip. L'Anse aux Meadows marks the first settlement in North America by European people.

Reconstructions of Viking buildings have been made at L'Anse aux Meadows from wood and earth.

Timbuktu, Mali

Camel caravans once gathered in the city of Timbuktu before crossing the Sahara Desert to trade in gold. Later the city grew into an important Islamic educational centre with three mosques. Today this inhabited city is under threat from desert sands that kill vegetation and damage buildings and water supplies.

The Djingareyber Mosque in Timbuktu was made in 1325 from earth mixed with straw and wood.

Brasília, Brazil

Brasília was designed to be a model city that would promote an ideal society. It was built in the 1950s in just four years, and became the capital of Brazil in 1960. Apartment buildings were limited to six storeys, and built in blocks called "superquadras". Wide avenues link different areas of the city, and motorways link the city with the rest of the country.

Brazil's new capital city was based on the shape of an aeroplane, with residential areas stretching out like wings from the central part of the city.

Buildings and Structures

Buildings and structures on the World Heritage List take many different forms. They tell us about the people who made them and the technologies they mastered.

Leaning Tower of Pisa, Italy

In 1172 a widow left sixty coins in her will to buy stone to build a bell tower for the cathedral in Pisa. The white marble tower was begun in 1173, but just five years later it began to lean because it was built on soft, marshy soil. By the late 20th century the tower was leaning 5 metres off-centre and was closed for years. It was recently reopened to the public.

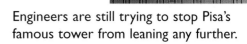

Engineers are still trying to stop Pisa's famous tower from leaning any further.

Great Wall, China

China's Great Wall winds for more than 5,000 kilometres. It is so long that it can be seen twisting across Earth from satellites in space. The wall was begun in 220 BC to defend the ancient Chinese Empire from invasions by tribes to the north. It was built 5.5 metres wide in parts to allow soldiers to march ten abreast.

Soldiers used the tall watchtowers along the wall to signal messages to each other.

Colosseum, Italy

Between AD 75 and 79 a huge stadium called the Colosseum was built in the centre of Rome to entertain the people of the Roman Empire. It opened in AD 80 with games that lasted for a hundred days. It could seat 50,000 people who watched the action in the main arena below them. Gladiators were kept in chambers below the stadium floor before they fought to the death in front of noisy crowds. Not only the Colosseum is a World Heritage Site in Rome – much of the ancient centre of the city is protected too.

The Colosseum was used to stage bloodthirsty gladiator contests for the entertainment of the ancient Romans.

The amphitheatre at Epidaurus is still used today.

Epidaurus Amphitheatre, Greece

The amphitheatre at Epidaurus was built in the 4th century BC and is still a magical place for plays to be performed. The auditorium is built into a hillside, with 14,000 seats surrounding the stage. If someone standing in the centre of the stage whispers, then the sound can be heard by someone sat in the back row. The amphitheatre lies within an area that is devoted to health and healing. The ancient Greeks believed going to the theatre would help people who were ill get better.

Pont du Gard, France

Pont du Gard is an enormous Roman aqueduct or bridge for carrying water. On the top level of the aqueduct was a water channel. This carried water 50 kilometres from a spring at Uzès to the Roman city of Nîmes. On the bottom level was a road that soldiers used to cross the River Gard.

Pont du Gard supplied the city of Nîmes with 20,000 tonnes of water every day.

Rice Terraces of the Philippine Cordilleras, Philippines

The Ifugao people have lived for more than 2,000 years in the rocky mountains of the Philippines, where heavy rainfall is often followed by landslides and flash floods. The Ifugao constructed rice terraces that rise from the valley floors to the mountain peaks. These terraces prevent the soil from being washed away by rains and flooding.

The rice terraces follow the contours of the mountains.

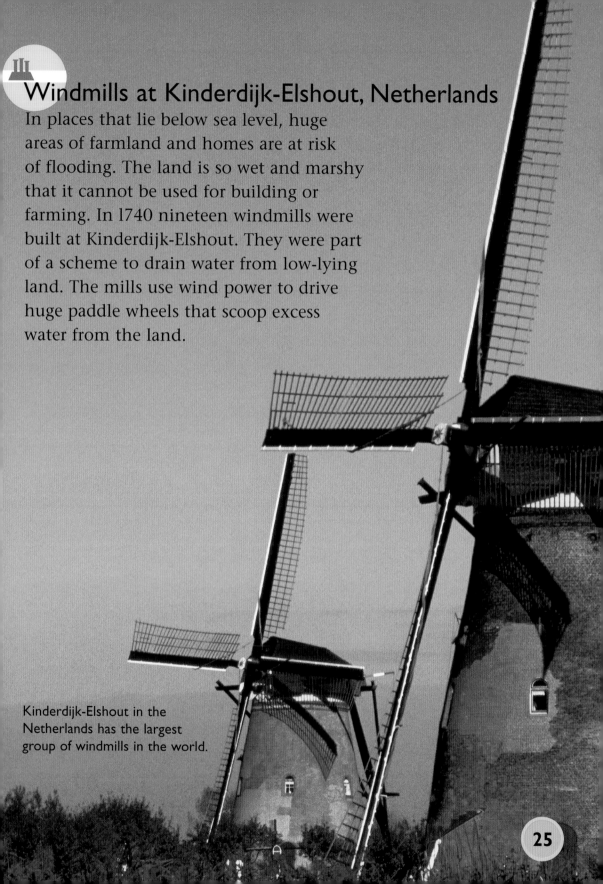

Windmills at Kinderdijk-Elshout, Netherlands

In places that lie below sea level, huge areas of farmland and homes are at risk of flooding. The land is so wet and marshy that it cannot be used for building or farming. In 1740 nineteen windmills were built at Kinderdijk-Elshout. They were part of a scheme to drain water from low-lying land. The mills use wind power to drive huge paddle wheels that scoop excess water from the land.

Kinderdijk-Elshout in the Netherlands has the largest group of windmills in the world.

Marvels and Mysteries

Past **civilizations** made stone circles, land art and burial places to express their beliefs. Over time, the purpose of these sites has sometimes become mysterious.

Rapa Nui National Park, Easter Island

Rapa Nui, or Easter Island, in the Pacific Ocean, is more than 3,000 kilometres west of Chile. It is one of the most isolated places on Earth, and is famous for the mysterious statues that stand guarding its coastline. In about AD 300 the Rapa Nui people settled there from Polynesia. They carved the statues, which are known as "moai", between the 10th and 16th centuries. They carved the huge heads from volcanic rock. Then they probably rolled them to the site on logs cut from the island's forests.

There are more than 600 moai on Rapa Nui. They range from 3 to 12 metres in height.

Giant Buddha of Leshan, China

The Giant Buddha is carved out of a hillside near Leshan in China. It was carved in the 8th century, and looks down at the point where three rivers meet. According to legend, the Giant Buddha was carved to calm an angry monster that lived in these rivers. It is in an area that is holy to Buddhists.

The Giant Buddha of Leshan is the largest stone sculpture of Buddha in the world.

Stonehenge, England

Stonehenge is a prehistoric stone monument that stands on Salisbury Plain in Wiltshire. It is made up of two huge stone circles. More stones lie across the tops to form arches, which frame the rising and setting Sun. **Archaeologists** believe Stonehenge may have been built as a place of worship to the Sun or to mark the cycle of the seasons like a giant calendar.

Stonehenge was built in about 3000 BC.

Great Pyramid of Giza, Egypt

In about 2550 BC the Great Pyramid was built for Pharaoh Khufu on the west bank of the River Nile. It is part of a large area called the "Pyramid Fields" where many pyramids, temples and tombs are found. It was built using more than 2 million blocks of stone, each weighing 2 tonnes. It took 100,000 workers twenty years to complete it. It is thought that workers used ropes and levers to lift the enormous blocks into place.

When the Great Pyramid was completed, it was 147 metres high. Today it is still the biggest stone building in the world. It is the grandest of all the pyramids, and the only one of the Seven Wonders of the Ancient World that is still standing.

Each of the four sides of the Great Pyramid are lined up with the compass points of north, south, east and west.

It took about 20,000 workers to build the Taj Mahal between 1631 and 1648.

Taj Mahal, India

On the banks of the River Jumna near Agra, India, stands the Taj Mahal. It was designed and built by Emperor Shah Jahan to house the tomb of his favourite wife. It is built of white marble and decorated with carved panels, gemstones and writings from the Koran, which is the holy book of the Islamic faith. A long canal leads towards the building, and its waters reflect the building's shimmering front.

Nasca Lines, Peru

Mysterious markings were first cut into the ground on the southern coast of Peru in the 1st century. They include shapes, figures, animals and plants. They are so large that they can only be seen clearly from the air.

The Nasca Lines include this spider, which is 50 metres wide.

Looking to the Future

World Heritage Sites are protected so no one can change them, dig them up or spoil them. But many sites remain endangered by nature and people. Natural disasters like heavy rains, forest fires and **erosion** can endanger sites. War, civil unrest and looting can also threaten sites. Crowds of visitors erode the land, wearing it away with their feet and their cars. They also bring noise, **pollution** and litter.

By protecting these sites, we are preserving them for future generations. That way, they too can marvel at the wonders of the Giant's Causeway, the Grand Canyon and the Nasca Lines.

Grand Canyon

Tourists in the future will also be able to enjoy World Heritage Sites.

Glossary

archaeologists	people who study people, cultures and objects from the past
civilizations	societies that developed skills, such as the arts and technology
crust	Earth's outer shell
cultural	associated with a society or civilization
endangered species	groups of animals in danger of dying out
erosion	wearing away of land by wind, water and ice, or by people
fossils	the remains of animals or plants from millions of years ago preserved in stone
geysers	springs that shoot boiling water and steam out of the ground
glaciers	slow-moving rivers of ice
habitat	the natural surroundings where plants or animals live
lava	hot, liquid rock that flows from a volcano when it erupts
molten	made into a liquid by heat; melted
pollution	damage to air, water and soil from harmful materials
savannah	flat, grassy land with few trees
table mountain	mountain with a flat top
UNESCO	United Nations Educational, Scientific and Cultural Organization

Index

Resources

Log on to UNESCO's website at *whc.unesco.org* to find out
more about UNESCO and other World Heritage Sites.

World Heritage in Young Hands (an educational resource kit
for teachers) is available from this website.